My Brother Jaz

For my mother Isabel.

JASPER

‘Reality, looked at steadily, is unbearable.’
– CS Lewis, *A Grief Observed*

1

CLASSY
CATS

Near 1 o'clock on the morning of 13 August 1987, a seventeen-year-old unemployed male was admitted to the Geelong Hospital suffering the trauma of a road accident. His skull was broken into five pieces. Both lobes of his brain were heavily contused. His ribs and clavicle were fractured. His spleen and liver were lacerated. As respirators and intravenous lines suspended him between life and death, other observations were made, including that his hair was light brown tinged blond and that his fingernails were short. But he was already more dead than alive. At 3.15 am, the resident medical officer declared extinct the life of Jasper Haigh. He was my brother.

I cannot tell how many times in the intervening years that I have considered documenting the story of that night, what led up to it, what ensued. Ten? Twenty? Probably more. Only once did I ever start—I could not proceed beyond two paragraphs. Another part of me wanted to set the events aside forever. For some time after, I even tried to forget the actual date. I worked to confuse myself, to spread the memory out, to flatten it into something I could roll over. I would refer to it as happening 'in August', I would fudge the year. I nearly succeeded. One day the date tumbled from my mother's mouth unbidden, and I realised I had known all along. Plus what good could writing about it do? Perhaps even less than none. It need hardly be said that my mother never recovered from the loss—a child predeceasing its parents disturbs the whole natural order, never again to be set right. Since then my mother and I have been more or less what we have in the world. Yet we have never discussed that night in detail, and barely even in the abstract.

I suspect it has impacted me in other ways, even as a journalist. Friends know of my pronounced, and frankly unreasonable, aversion to autobiographical writings. The sentimental gush of life tales. The sickly sweetness of memoir. The humblebraggart columnists who festoon newspapers. Autofiction—kill me now. People making a fuss. People seeking attention. The ease, the facility, even the relish with which they detain us. I know by heart Will Rogers' definition of memoir: 'When you put down the good things you ought to have done, and leave out the bad ones you did do'.

At the same time, trauma, individual and intergenerational, has been a recurrent subject in my non-fiction. I shrink from the cliché that I've masked my own pain by superimposing the pain of others. But I am moved in its presence. I feel like I get it, except my own. Perhaps placing myself at the service of my stories has been an unconscious turning of the attention from myself. I was a journalist more than a decade before I used a personal pronoun, in writing up an interview, and only because every other construction of the sentence did not work; I remember flinching; it was like knowing sin for the first time.

It happened that my brother died in the week my first book was published; to him my second book was dedicated. But in forty-nine subsequent books I've never been able to do better, never felt up to the task of addressing my life's gravest loss. I am fifty-eight; Jasper would now be fifty-four. The former I can deal with; the latter is beyond my comprehension. Sometimes my fourteen-year-old daughter C reminds me of my brother—in the way she smiles, the way she holds her head, her profile, her eyes—and just in that instant it cuts me that there is this uncle she never knew. The sense of Jasper is always there, out of sight, but bulking darkly like a submerged continent.

As I sit here, I can feel myself heaping up obstacles to what I'm about to write. I'm veering between the objections that what I can say is either of no conceivable interest to anyone, or the kind of confessional nonsense I have always deprecated. The least of them is the possibility that people will think I'm weird, because people in my trade already think that—a contrarian, a refusenik, difficult, trouble. I'm saddled with that reputation, and there's no changing it even if I wanted to. But I also know that in the past few years, I've found myself backing towards an effort to discharge this story, just to see if it makes me feel any differently.

I cannot tell when this started. There was no specific event, except perhaps that the surges and eddies of my relationship with D loosened my sedimented sadness. Five or so years ago, I encountered a book by Richard Beard, whom I knew as the author of a very humane and funny book about rugby, *Muddied Oafs*. *The Day That Went Missing* could hardly have been more different: it was Beard's account of the drowning of his younger brother Nicky on a family holiday in Cornwall in August 1978. So utter was his family's denial of the loss that, having paid in advance, they continued the holiday. It instilled the custom of a lifetime:

> Since the age of eleven I've dodged the pain, generally kept feeling to a minimum as a pre-caution against sudden disaster. I've sleepwalked through pre-forgotten days. The project was *not* to feel, as encouraged in that extra week.

A step: if I could not address parallel events in my own life, I could at least watch someone try to address theirs. For, nearly forty years on, his life fraying and his marriage crumbling, Beard went in search of 'the emotional content in a lost true event', interrogating family members, tracking down witnesses, drawing on official records. Reading the book meant breaking my own resistance to consuming autobiography. Interestingly, Beard observed that life had shaped his own partiality to fiction: made-up stories had proven easier for him, just as other people's stories had proven easier for me. It was both a very good book and very difficult to read. I complemented it, quietly, with other canonical books about mourning, like CS Lewis's *A Grief Observed* and RK Narayan's *The English Teacher*. This was my shit; I would get through it my way.

Then, one day, tramping round my old neighbourhood, I saw that the Canning Street house in which

I had lived those many years ago was for sale, and open for inspection. Emboldened a little by Beard perhaps, I walked in. I knew exactly where I was headed: straight to the kitchen where, in the early hours of 13 August 1987, I answered consecutive phone calls: my mother telling me that Jasper was seriously injured; my mother confirming he had died. The wall phone was gone; the wall remained. The space was exactly as I remembered, even the pattern of the nails in the wood at which I stared so hard, as if I was biting down on a bullet. I could see the 21-year-old me again, so young, barely shaving. I had just finished my cadetship. I had just bought my first suit for the launch of my first book. My mother was saying, 'What about the launch? What about the launch?' And I was telling her not to worry, it was nothing, absolutely nothing. It was a fucking book—who cared?

In a way the visit was reassuring. It was there. It was all still there. I had not blanked those memories: they were parked; they were accessible. I had always worried I would forget. Indeed, I had taken precautions. I had one of Jasper's shirts in my wardrobe. I had a boy's belt stamped with his name in my drawer, from a day trip to Sovereign Hill. They were incorporated into my daily regime. I subconsciously greeted them while dressing every morning. They were an admonition not to forget. Maybe they had worked. The past was not a blur. It was all eerily clear.

But incomplete. After the accidental pilgrimage to Canning Street, a long-held thought recurred. Had my brother had an inquest? As a journalist, I have developed a profound fascination with the genre of inquests—the state capturing a moment of extremity in the life of its people. Again, make of that what you will. I had read thousands of inquests, but never the inquest most meaningful to me. That was assuming it existed, because I would need to lodge an inquiry with the Coroners Court to find out, all the while without investing too deep a hope; there might, after all, be no such document. I equivocated. I tried, as I once had with the date, to forget the idea, to tamp the notion down.

Some months passed. And then, one day, I knew that the only way to overcome my interest was to indulge it. I made an application. The wait was long—six further slow-passing months. First came a confirmation. Yes, there was a file; no, it had still to be located. Did I wish to see it? I could hardly exist in the same world as a record of my brother's death—the proof it happened, as it were—without consulting it. Retrieval took further months, which I rationalised: so much time had I waited, a little more scarcely mattered. And who knew? The file might be a handful of pages or even empty. Then about eighteen months ago, an email heralded the arrival of a 41-page PDF titled 'Jasper Haigh Reports'.

D was there as I clicked on it. I started reading the pages … and I finished. I had expected to pore over the contents, to dwell on them, to turn them over and over for revelations. I found I could not. I saw statements, headings, words; they were like patterns or glyphs. My eye glanced off the pages; it was as if the paper and ink would not yield to my eye. I'm conscious that I'm taking too long to get where I'm heading, and to a putative reader feel apologetic, but I have to narrate this step. On the contents of 'Jasper Haigh Reports', it seemed like my attention could make no indentation; I felt the decades-long habit of rendering the facts an unthreatening fuzz against which it was not too painful to brush.

Five minutes later, all I felt was a need to convince myself that the reading experience had not been so bad, that these were mere documents, confirmations of existing knowledge, reinforcements of the status quo. Another part of me knew this was not true, that I had been unable to make sense of them, that maybe I was deliberately missing something. But when a lie is important enough, one must fall in with it. D was solicitous. Was there anything that stood out, she wondered, anything I wanted to take further? To placate her, I pronounced myself satisfied. She didn't understand, but how could she? I did not. All I could think was no, this is not the day; no, I am not ready. One day, maybe, I will be. But not yet, not yet.

Another six months went by, a year. Vivacious D vanished, probably bored of the brooding figure I am ever on the verge of becoming. Who wanted to spend time with a guy like that? I didn't want to spend time with a guy like that. This had consequences. 'When you're without a woman it's astonishing how quickly you become loathsome to yourself,' observed Martin Amis. 'It is astonishing, too, how quickly this news gets around.' At least there was work, stimulant and analgesic. No matter how I have been feeling in my life, work has always been there; I may even work hardest when saddest.

Then, one night in Sydney in January 2024, I found myself in a circle of friends and scholars, where the talk turned to archives and our favourite finds. To the nearest person, I confided that I had perused my brother's inquest. Her eyes widened. What had happened to him? I imagine she meant what the inquest had revealed, yet I reached instinctively not for what was on paper, whose surface I had hardly scratched, but what was in my head: my own personal inquest, which I knew from my visit to Canning Street was still fully stocked. I did not say much and steered the subject away. The conversation rolled on.

But something previously tight had loosened. I excused myself. I felt the urge to write. I had only the vaguest of ideas, of themes. Document versus memory in a traumatic event? Sure, whatever. On this subject where it related to my brother, after all, I was the world's number one authority. Back at my digs, where it was after midnight, I opened my laptop. I would have to write fast, I realised, to get to a point where it became impossible not to finish, before the pall of mourning or futility shut the light out entirely. And that … well, that brings us smack-bang into the present. This is where I'm sitting right this minute, on a cottage's verandah with a screen glowing emptily in front of me. What now? There are so many potential beginnings to the story of my brother's death, but I don't have time to sweat on the right one, so I won't wait. If this is to be done, it must be *right fucking now.*

2

P

P

It doesn't feel right to call him Jasper. He was always Jaz, just as I was always Gid. I was older by four years, which as anyone will tell you is a sizeable difference. He was born just after we moved to Geelong, into an old weatherboard with a fibro extension. I had a tiny bedroom barely big enough for a single bed; Jaz inherited a larger room partly because it started as a nursery. I don't recall any jealousy as I was confident of my irreducible seniority in years, and secure in my parents' love.

About the latter, I was mistaken. I don't recall anyone explaining why, when I was six and Jaz two, our parents were divorcing, or even that they were. The word, in my memory, was never used, and it is easy to imagine the taboo on it in what was a glorified country town. I do remember following my father into the driveway one afternoon. Where was he going? I asked. Away for a while, he replied. I did not see him for another fifteen years. I have seen him on only three occasions since. It's at least a decade since we shared as much as an email.

I proved, or so I thought, capable of normalising the experience, becoming one of those older sons whom divorce turns into a kind of proxy husband. I sat in the passenger seat of our car, Jaz in the back. I accompanied my mother to social occasions, Jaz remaining at home. I felt grown up before my time. I *was* grown up before my time. The proviso 'or so I thought' is a recent and, I confess, rather reluctant reflection. When my daughter C was six, she asked had I any item from when I was six. Rummaging in some old boxes I found an elaborate texta drawing dated 1972 depicting my parents. My father was descending the stairs of an airliner, approaching my mother's welcoming hug. 'Mumy!' read the speech balloon. I was imagining my parents reuniting after my father's absence on a business trip; it was actually from that trip he returned with the mistress who became his second wife.

Clearly I had been invested in the idea of my parents loving each other; I cannot recall actively reconciling myself to the idea that they did not. I merely 'got on with things', and for as long as I can remember that is what I have done. I am good at it—so good that most of the time I am unaware of the effort involved. In a sense I trained with a master. This is my mother. She is tough, uncomplaining, practical, reliable. She has had more to deal with than I ever did and remains a stranger to self-pity. I'll never be as good at that as she is, but I can try.

Our mother called us 'the boys'. In conversation, on the phone, in letters, we were always 'the boys'. It's been so long since I heard or thought of that plural, yet it impressed on my mind that we were a pair, side by side at tea time, together in the trees we climbed, watching the same cartoons and always coupled in photographs. In these, you might not necessarily have picked us as brothers.

I was slim, biddable, bookish; Jaz broader, more rugged, more physical. He made friends easily; I did not. I did well at school; he did not. I liked wearing ties; he rode a bike and a skateboard. While the age gap removed any sense of competition, it did not preclude comparison. My mother had cause for pride in me and cause for reflection with Jaz: more adventurous, less articulate, he was an archetype of the 'boy who needed his father'. But his father lived in the US and experienced no corresponding need for either of his sons.

Jaz and I were close, in very particular ways. There is not nearly the literature round brothers that there is around sisters. For a male, a brother acts as a kind of extension of the self, an additional affirming arm, an extra set of hands, with an assumption of reliability. You add up to more than two. It interested me as we grew how little we needed to say to each other to understand exactly what was going on inside us—our outward differences made this knack for grunting assent more remarkable. I guess it's this kind of unspoken communion that underlies the modern abbreviation 'bro', raising male friendship to the status of blood tie. I guess that because I really hate it. I love my friends, but none of them is on par with my brother.

I won't attempt my brother's biography here; it would be a travesty. Jaz lived seventeen years, hardly long enough to have a story. The nub of it is that as he entered puberty, his undischarged confusion was enlarged by size and strength. He played up. He got in trouble. And he talked more about our father, whom he struggled to remember. What was our father like? Was he a good guy? Would Jaz like him? I hadn't a clue; I remembered him only poorly myself.

A lot went on in this period that my mother rather kept from me—although what am I saying here? Of course, she did: I was a boy myself. I remember a few years ago I was invited to speak to a Melbourne club by a man who identified himself and whose name I remembered as one of Jaz's senior teachers. When I told my mother, her face hardened. 'Just another one of the upright, respectable men who washed their hands of Jaz,' she said. She remembered him saying, 'Go home, Mrs Haigh. It doesn't get any better.' His defence might be that he was right.

So Jaz lost his way. Most of us do at some stage, but Jaz could not find his way back. Other schools rejected him—and in a country town, a boy could get a reputation. He resisted school, expressing instead an

interest in living with my father; after all, why should he not? It was, perhaps predictably, a disaster.

In advance of Jaz's visit, our father demanded a psychiatrist's letter that Jaz was 'safe'. Once Jaz arrived, our father managed to absent himself 'on business' most of three bleak winter months of the stay. 'Our father': I'm deploying that phrase with a heavy-handed irony. But he was, wasn't he?

So Jaz languished in this alien house on the other side of the world playing cards with our father's new mother-in-law, and soon was chafing to return to Australia. In 1984, aged eighteen, I went to work as a cadet journalist in Melbourne. In 1985, aged fifteen, Jaz went to work in a wrecker's yard in Newcastle. The job had been lined up by my uncle on the logic that Jaz might then seek an automotive apprenticeship. Jaz, it was reasoned, was 'good with his hands'—that anachronism foisted on boys whom the educational mill could not accommodate.

The move was at best a qualified success. My brother and my uncle didn't get on, so Jaz moved into the YMCA. But it brought us closer. We wrote each other. His letters from 'the Y' were anecdotal, sardonic. In some ways, though we were separated, these couple of years were the best of our brotherly lives. We developed a mutual respect to go with our mutual origins. I was impressed with him: he had been dealt a bad hand; he had ridden out a tough time; he appeared to be 'getting on with things'—our family's natural vein.

When Jaz returned to Geelong and moved back into his childhood bedroom, it was clear that the experience had changed him in other ways. Newcastle had put him in the path of alcohol and dope—he carried a plant of his own in a custom-made box. He was taller than me by now, considerably fitter, and had lost weight from an exercise regime—a sharper eye than mine might have detected an eating disorder, for he teased me about my physique and food habits. When he stayed with me in Melbourne, sleeping on my couch, I found him good company. But, bigger and stronger, he was also potentially bad company. The police became regular visitors to my mother's home, and suggested that she declare Jaz 'uncontrollable', rendering him suitable for a 'training centre'—another hateful euphemism, this for juvenile jail. Another day a drug dealer turned up on my mother's doorstep calling in a debt.

I know of all this only in passing. In fact, after decades of half-finished conversations, I know probably only a fraction of what there is to know. I know how my mother encouraged Jaz to see a psychiatrist and how seldom he went. I know how my mother would not keep alcohol in the house and hid her jewellery in her car's glove compartment, little attempts to keep temptation at bay. Even if I knew more, I'd probably refrain from saying it. A journalist might deem it relevant; for once I am not in that capacity. Lots of young males pass through a stage of cutting up rough, getting in strife, and a stage it remains, sometimes recalled in later years even with a touch of fondness. Later I would resent well-meant mutterings like 'He was never going to make old bones'. It made things worse not better, and those things were already awful.

3

OK, it's getting on to dawn, and I'm going to click on 'Jasper Haigh Reports' for the first time in more than a year, during which time it has been sitting on my desktop. I can see that it opens with my mother's statement that, on the night of 12 August 1987, she arrived home from a class she was taking at the Gordon Institute to find Jaz 'on the phone to a girl'. This was not apparently an uncommon occurrence despite his variable humours. Jaz, she consented, 'would be moody and in a depressed state occasionally'.

My mum called out goodnight, locked the back door, went to bed and apparently slept. That meant she did not hear Jaz, having earlier pocketed a spare set of car keys, climb out his bedroom window at about 11 pm, and guide our blue Ford Telstar, registration CEO796, down the driveway. He drove to a share house in Sharp Street, Newtown, owned by the Durlings, whose son Andrew was a mate. Andrew was out, but Andrew's sister Julie and a young couple, Alistair Craik and Natalie Alsop, were there. The trio had been watching television, playing records and drinking port from a cask all evening. They were in their early twenties, and their statements reek of youthful indirection and listlessness: 'Towards midnight I was getting pretty drunk but I can still recall what occurred,' Natalie insisted.

Although Jaz had been looking for Andrew, he joined Natalie and Alistair in front of the television. Alistair had met my brother on only half a dozen occasions, but felt able to offer observations of him:

> I knew that JASPER had been living in NSW for over a year and had been in Geelong only the last couple of months and the last couple of times I had seen him I felt he was in a depressed state a number of times. JASPER was quite often depressed and he would have some days where he was quite alright and other days when he would just mope or sit and look depressed.

Alistair thought nothing of it when Jaz said, 'I've got the car', believing he was older than eighteen and had a NSW licence.

We decided to go for a drive to the coast, possibly down to Lorne but we had no definite plans. We were just going to drive and NATALIE and I were going to drink. NATALIE and I put the cask and beer in the car and I sat in the front with JASPER driving. NATALIE sat in the back behind me. I recognised the car as a Telstar sedan. JASPER said it was his mum's. It appeared to me as though he had permission to have the car but in my state I didn't give it another thought.

JASPER drove down Sharp Street towards LaTrobe Terrace and turned left. I can't recall what his driving was like at that stage.

We did a 'U' turn and headed south towards Fyans Street and turned left at Fyans Street and as he approached the intersection with Moorabool Street, he was driving very fast and I think we went through a red light at that intersection. JASPER'S driving scared me a bit then, I got the impression he was trying to show off.

JASPER said that he needed petrol before we left and we needed cigarettes anyway.

> We noticed that the service station was closed and we continued up Moorabool Street and I can't remember where we turned but the next thing we were heading north on Gheringhap Street approaching an intersection at a fast speed.
>
> The lights were red and I could see a car's headlights approaching the intersection from the right. JASPER didn't slow down, and I could see that we were going to collide with this other vehicle. I did not say or do anything and JASPER drove straight through the red light and it was all blank at that moment.

Reading now, and I've just realised why I failed to comprehend this statement the first time round—why it would not go in. Yes, there's the pall of bored suggestibility about the plan. Yes, there's the whiff of youthful bravado in Jaz's driving. But I keep looking at those sentences where Alistair Craik is describing how he could see the red traffic signal and the headlights of the car, a BMW, approaching from the right, *from his passenger seat*. Jaz must have done the same. It did not stop him. There is a hint he even accelerated. The BMW barrelled straight into the driver's side door of the Telstar.

And I've just had a memory—in fact, I can't deny I've always been aware of it. Some years later, in my foggy, confused, depressed state, I began to see the same psychiatrist my mother had tried to encourage my brother to see: a kindly, compassionate man called Marcus Benjamin, with whose sons I had gone to school. One day we were discussing my family's history, and he had recourse to the phrase 'when your brother killed himself'.

'But Marcus,' I said, 'Jaz had an accident.'

'Gideon,' Marcus said patiently, 'your brother killed himself.'

~

It's raining, but I've just returned from a walk. I often walk when I have something to turn over in my head. I have been thinking about the streets down which Jaz drove, which we knew well, because my grandmother lived in a flat on Gheringhap Street: she would have been asleep 100 metres away as the Telstar approached. I have been thinking how for at least twenty years of visits to Geelong after Jaz's death I would avoid that intersection with McKillop Street, and how one day I knew it was close, knew it was on my route and decided to pass through it.

It was daytime, but otherwise the streetscape was unchanged since 1987. I remained for at least a quarter of an hour, watching the lights change from green to red and back again, as the traffic moved frictionlessly. The streets are wide. The views are unimpeded. It is the simplest of crossroads, this crossroads of my family's life. Had I acknowledged even then the truth in Marcus's remark, but been unable to assimilate it? Had I seen Craik's recollection when first I read 'Jasper Haigh Reports' but convinced myself I hadn't? But pardon my parking these self-interrogations for the moment. I have left my brother dying.

When Alistair Craik came to, he was bleeding from nose and face:

> JASPER's head was on my knee and I could hear him moaning. I said 'JASPER are you all right?' but he just moaned. I turned and said 'NATALIE are you all right?' She said 'Yes.'

Moaning: they never tell you that, do they? When those accident scenes that are the staples of evening news are aired, one sees only flashing lights and scurrying paramedics. What about the sounds of an accident—of excruciated pain, of groggy inquiry, of hurried conversation? Maybe that's why my mother always turns off the television when there is an accident. She can hear the moaning. From now on, I suspect I will too.

Also at the scene were the driver of the BMW, Wendy Maddern, and the Mercedes behind her, Rex Gorrell, her de facto. As the marques suggest, they were members of the Geelong *beau monde.* Gorrell owned a big car yard and The Source restaurant, where the couple had been dining earlier—a posh, big occasion place where, it happened, my mother had taken me on my eighteenth birthday. Maddern, thankfully, was little injured; once he was satisfied she was all right, Gorrell seems to have grown rather detached:

> I could see that there was a girl and some other people in the car and it was obvious that they were injured. I could see the girl was slumped over and I went back to my car to call for an ambulance on my car phone.

When the police arrived, he made a point of advising them: 'If I were you I'd check the inside of that Telstar. It smells of alcohol.'

Reading this back all these years later, I feel a welling fury. That was my dying brother, not 'other people'! Bully for your sodding car phone, and for telling the cops how to do their jobs! I know full well that this is utterly unfair, but I cannot stop feeling it. I am assuaged a little by the fact that his prompt action ensured the arrival of an ambulance within ten minutes—Geelong Hospital was actually less than a mile away—and that paramedics extricated Jaz quickly by cutting his seatbelt away.

Half an hour after the accident, Jaz was in the intensive care unit. Ten minutes later, my mother was awoken by the ringing of a bedside telephone telling her so. So I shouldn't be distracted by Rex Gorrell; it's my mother who matters now; now and evermore. For the police, she covered her journey in only three sentences.

> I went to the garage and saw that the car was gone and I realised what had happened.
>
> I called for a taxi and checked in JASPER'S room and saw that the window was open.

> Shortly after that I arrived at the Geelong Hospital where I spoke to the Police and hospital staff, and I then identified the body of my son, JASPER, at the intensive care unit of the Hospital.

This just about breaks me. Because here's the thing: my brother had been born in Geelong Hospital. I find myself thinking of my hopeful parents taking that first journey in, probably in our secondhand cream Datsun in 1969; of my abandoned mother taking that second journey in a cab less than eighteen years later because her car was stolen. Her son is not yet a body; Jaz is still my brother. Her first call to me, in fact, is explicit about this: Jaz is injured, badly. But the possibilities are not foreclosed. His heart still beats. His tense is still present. And now I am in the story.

~

The phone does not ring at 1.30 am without good reason. I had been asleep in the front room of the house in Canning Street, but sensed the urgency immediately.

I had last seen Jaz a few days earlier. He had come from Geelong; we had gone to Melba's Hotel for gristly steaks and generous jugs of beer. It had been a typical conversation between us. Our mother was a saint, our father was a cunt; we felt affirmed in sharing this. My brother was looking good, and I told him so. 'You're looking shithouse,' he joked. 'You need to take care of yourself better. You're going to seed!' As he had sloped off, dope plant box under his arm, I'd thought of how the passage of time had shrunk that four-year gap, so vast in our youths. We had both left home for jobs, and I imagined us strangely *embarked.* I pondered what we'd been through, what we might become. What *he* was thinking, I cannot reach back far enough to speculate. Was he depressed, as Alistair Craik suspected? Was he self-destructive, as Marcus insisted? My first thought when my mother called, at any rate, I know full well: he *must* live; he's made it; we've both made it; this is so wrong, this is so *unfair.* And I do something I find embarrassing to admit, even after all this time, even acknowledging that it is standard. I pray to God, whom I have never had any use for; I bargain with God, whom I do not believe in; I offer myself in my brother's place; I promise never again to do anything bad, to be a better person, even to accept Him into my life. I hate this admission, because it is at once such a cliché, and also renders me so transparent to myself. This is what everyone does. Why wasn't I good enough to find a better way? Why hadn't I been smart enough to plan for this? A Pascal's wager—I should have made a Pascal's wager. My housemate is away. The house is silent. I can hear my own breathing. I can feel my mind racing, but in dizzying circles, until it almost corkscrews into the floor; an hour passes that feels like a minute.

At about 3.20 am the phone rings again. I snatch it from the cradle. 'He's dead, Gid,' says my mother. 'Jaz's dead.' She is apologetic about turning off the life support but had no choice. She tells me she has consented to the harvesting of my brother's corneas. The permission slip forms part of 'Jasper Haigh Reports'. There is her signature—firm, legible and so recognisable from my childhood, on drivers' licences, on cheque butts, on notes to school giving permission and excusing absence. How did she do it? How did she have such presence of mind, such fortitude? Still, we hardly know what to say and do. Our conversation about the book launch is the first of many absurd diversions—absurd yet they seem so necessary. None are stranger than what I do next.

I dress and start walking into town, heading vaguely for Spencer Street. There is a rise on Rathdowne Street where the Museum now sits and where you seem to look down on the beckoning city, and my eyes take in what feels like a snapshot. This is now. This is here. My life will never be the same. I must remember this moment, what I'm doing, how I'm feeling. But my purpose setting off so early is … to pass by my office en route to the railway station in order to file a record review. I have undertaken to write about the new Echo & the Bunnymen album for that Friday's entertainment guide. It must done or … or what? I don't know. The heavens will fall? I know it is stupid, I know it is illogical and that the review's absence could easily be dealt with. But as I hunker over my video display unit in the darkened newsroom of *The Age*, I am reassured by knowing that at least this is within my capabilities. I have failed to stop my brother from dying, but I can lodge this review so my editor need not worry.

Since then I have written many reviews; what I do next I have never done again. I descend into the subterranean court of Spencer Street station to await the 5 am train to Geelong, and there it is, by which I have passed numberless times, an old-fashioned photo booth. If I want to capture this moment, this feeling, what better way than a photograph? The booth allows four photographs at intervals. In the first I look stunned, slack-jawed and empty-eyed; by the fourth I have shaped my mouth into a rictus of demented mirth. Am I checking that I still know how? Am I trying to work out whether this now feels different? Am I … yes, I am just a fucking mess, an absolute fucking mess. I'm feeling weak, light-headed, tremulous. A shame my brother's not around to roll me a joint. A shame my brother's now dead. Aged seventeen. Lying in a hospital mortuary, with his stove-in head and his own empty eye sockets. And here I am, on my way to see him the last time, having written a record review and pocketed a self-portrait. What am I doing? What am I now to do?

4

Next I remember I'm walking through Geelong, away from the station, bound for the hospital—that venue of Jaz's birth and death. You know the feeling you get from approaching some unavoidable dread, that every step is necessarily narrowing the distance remaining while shortening the time available and dissolving the safety margin? I have that feeling. Presently the brick exterior looms, and I ascend the ramp into emergency, where I ask the duty nurse if I can see my brother, as though I've come to drop off a couple of magazines and a bunch of grapes.

The nurse explains that I have come to the wrong place at the wrong time but, when I state his name insistently, studies her records and looks back with understanding. She's afraid it's not possible, and I am starting to grasp the reality that I no longer have a brother to see, that it's too late, for *everything*. That future I had glimpsed just a few days earlier? It is sealed off. We will not be advancing together through the decades, he four years in arrears. Our paths have parted. I am on my own.

The cab driver who drives me to our family home is of the jolly kind. People must have told him that a cheery word brightens every passenger's day. When I explain that I'm tired, he chirps, 'Nothing a shower and a shave won't fix!' So I rehearse the words aloud for the first time, 'Oh, I don't know about that. You see, my brother's just died.' The silence that descends at least ensures a few minutes' respite.

Some things are already in motion. My mother is practical even in the presence of death. Within minutes of my arriving, there is a knock at the door: funeral directors, promptly summoned. We convene in our sitting room with its sliding doors, floral couch, velvety armchairs and tasteful artworks discussing the range of available coffins, with all their various features. Half-hinged lid? High-quality lacquer finish? Here we are, as the Haighs have always done, 'getting on with it'. Were it permissible, we might perform the burial ourselves in the backyard.

Then I do something useful—useful and terrible. Our car has now been dragged to a police lot. When our family friends Julie and Ann arrive with open-handed offers of help, they drive me. We walk up and down until I spy our numberplate. The Telstar is almost unrecognisable—the concaved door swinging loose, the pillar destroyed, the interior sparkling with broken windscreen and liberally streaked with my brother's blood, which has dried in the trims and pooled in the centre console. The passenger door is locked, so I reach in from the other side to stretch for the glove box. In doing so I put my knee on the driver's seat in which my brother has not long before been fatally injured. I smell the faint whiff of petrol. I feel the shards of glass through my jeans. I find the drawstring bag containing my mother's jewellery and also extract her golf clubs from the boot. I cannot believe I did it, but I did.

I'm at the point right now where I just wonder what the hell I'm doing. Not in 1987: that had a rationale. In 2024: I'm sitting here almost but not quite overwhelmed by the futility of what I'm writing. Who is this for? What is there remaining to be said? I'm hating the claim I am making to importance. I do not feel important; I feel powerless, inconsequential. Why did I even start this? The only reason I can think of is that it has to be done. It can't remain unwritten, just as I could never leave Jaz unremembered. I have myself to change, and how am I to do this unless I examine this defining event in my life face on? Maybe it will alter nothing, but if I do not do it, how will I know?

This takes me back to what I was thinking in 1987, which was: I am going to spare myself nothing; I will do whatever is necessary; I will not look away. Because here I am a day later, with my mother, at the funeral home. She is doing the paperwork, efficiently executing her unmistakable signature. Nothing is going to stop me seeing the body. I walk in alone. The casket is on the other side of the room, maybe fifteen paces away. It is dark, it is panelled and it is open. I am going to say goodbye to my brother because what if I don't and regret it?

But I don't say goodbye. I feel myself crumbling. 'Oh Jaz, what have you gone and done now?' I ask him. 'Now there's only half of us. We were "the boys", weren't we? Now I'm just *the boy*.' My heart is racing, my breath is short, sweat is beading on my forehead. To get through, I concentrate on the aesthetics of the encounter. I've honestly never gazed so intently on a human form. I know he has been stuck back together like a broken statue, but I am almost overcome by Jaz's beauty. I am transfixed by his skin's chalky paleness, fascinated by all his head's contours and features, astonished at the length of his eyelashes, the precision of his tear ducts, the perfection of his earlobes. His scalp features a parting straighter than anything my brother ever achieved in life—up close I can see the follicles from which the hair has been teased this way and that. There must be hairspray keeping it in place. The people who do this work are accomplished professionals; it really does *look* like my brother. But, of course, it's not *him*. It is a deserted hull of flesh repaired by hand, stabilised by chemicals and draped in a suit of clothes he would never have worn in a million years. And it is *still*. My God, you have never experienced stillness until you have seen a loved one's body, from which everything that made them has departed, and nothing that you cherished remains. I lean over, kiss his forehead. It is cold as marble. And I walk out. 'Was it OK?' my mother asks. 'Fine,' I say.

My friend W comes from Melbourne. I need someone; I need something. W is a fount of kindness. We take a walk round the neighbourhood. To Dunsmore: the road where Jaz and his friends rode their bikes. To Mary's place: she was the lady whose enormous dog we walked for 80 cents a pop, me being vaguely terrified, Jaz handling it with ease. Through the bottom terrace of Jaz's primary school, on to the bus stop where on a previous visit I'd noticed among all the vivid, scatalogical graffiti, a tiny biro scrawl: 'JHaigh rools'. From his letters I knew his handwriting well. 'JHaigh rools': that peculiar mix of adolescent bombast and hesitancy, now signifying his barely having had time or scope to make a mark. I point it out to W. One day, it occurs to me, a council worker will come along and diligently scrub away all the defacement here, including my brother's last earthly testament. Every day, in fact, Jaz will slip away from me a little more. W asks how I'm feeling. I repeat that I'm fine.

Then guess who materialises? There he is, in our sitting room, a decade and a half since the last sighting in these parts: our father. A mediocrity, a nobody, nothing to me. I'll give him this: he looks gaunt, broken. And, I think, rightly so. I do what I suspect Jaz would have wanted me to. I tell our father what we thought of him and what I think of him still, that he squibbed the most basic requirement of paternal duty—turning up. There are other people in the room, but I don't care. This is on him. This whole shitshow is down to his absence from Jaz's life.

Does it feel good? Does it feel pointless? I don't experience any pride while taking a bit of skin off his worthless hide or enjoy any karmic satisfaction afterwards; the words feel almost like they utter themselves, or maybe they come from Jaz through me. My father breaks down. I hear his soft sobs, understand that he's a father who has lost his son, and I steel myself to feel *nothing*. And at this I am starting to get good.

The next day I give the eulogy at the funeral. It is my most public role in this sequence of events; many people afterwards will praise my courage and dignity; of it I have almost no memory at all. I have begun closing those windows into my soul that events had thrown open. Perhaps they had only been narrowly open before; pretty soon they will be shut altogether.

~

The day after the funeral I return to *The Age*. But I don't just go to work, I go looking for it. I tell my boss that not only am I *fine,* even *good to go,* but that I will welcome extra duties. 'Keep me busy,' I say, and so he does. Five weeks later, when the share market crashes, I feel exhilarated. Stocks are plunging. Savings are being wiped out. That the market is shedding a fifth of its value in a day feels curiously apposite to one who has just lost a third of his family in an hour.

It is not so long ago, but these reflections reinforce a view that the world was then a pitiless place in the presence of death. We mock this age's mushy soft-heartedness, but support for the bereaved back then was meagre and expertise non-existent. All I can remember is the appearance in our bookshelf of Elisabeth Kübler-Ross's *On Death and Dying.* I never read it. 'Have you had a good rest?' says her headmaster when my mother resumes teaching Grade 5 after a week. There is no counselling, no cushioning and no warning at the potential pitfalls of trying to move on too quickly.

For three months, the door to my brother's bedroom remains closed until at last my mother steels herself to clean it. When she goes to make the old single bed with the old tartan bedspread, what does she find behind it but Jaz's nail clippings. Remember how the hospital staff noted that his fingernails were short? Now that Jaz's body has been cremated, these are the last organic remnant of her second son. She agonises about whether to keep them; she decides eventually not to. She has only very recently told me this story.

We have an expression in our family: the 'PBMs'. The 'poor-bloody-mes' are those who crave sympathy, indulge in self-pity—the people from whom we separate ourselves. The abbreviation is credited to my aunt, who through a bad marriage and chronic ill-health was a formidable mother and an accomplished professional. But I was a conscript Spartan. My chief coping mechanism was giving up. I remembered my brother's joking reproach that I was going to seed, except that it no longer sounded a joke, for I felt base, impure, corrupt and guilty—fucking unremittingly guilty. Guilt doesn't need a reason—there is always a free-floating supply in the vicinity. But guilt does deserve a sentence, a penance. Mine was to a steady elimination of pleasure, a remorseless rededication to bare survival. I gave up alcohol. I gave up meat. I sacrificed playing sport and listening to music. I gave up, frankly, sex: the rest of my twenties would be an erotic blank. It was like I'd been bisected and reassembled arbitrarily, pleasure centres cauterised.

Even my sartorial standards slumped. As a boy, as I said, I'd had a precocious affection for ties; from 13 August 1987, I wore them only under acutest sufferance. Shaving I could handle only every other day, and I notice that Lewis in *A Grief Observed* surrendered to the same apathy: 'What does it matter now whether my cheek is rough or smooth?' He likened himself to a bone-weary man in want of an extra blanket on a cold night who ultimately would 'rather lie there shivering than get up and find one'. That suit of mine languished. What was there to dress up for, to look neat in aid of? I became a legendarily informal dresser; only I understood, at a level almost but not quite unconscious, how studied that insouciance was, how those T-shirts and duffle coats were in a way my mourning clothes. I have bought one suit since, for a job it was politely suggested I wear one. It cost $6 and I would have paid no more.

I even gave up thinking, at least where my predicament was concerned. Before 13 August 1987, I had been an assiduous, rather overwrought diarist. Introspection seemed exactly what an acute, sensitive, literary young man should be doing. But at the very instant they might have served some purpose, the diaries petered out. Some years ago I discovered a box of old exercise books I had filled with personal scrawlings and found that my last entry actually stopped mid-sentence, as though I'd suddenly dropped from a window ledge. I hazarded to read them, of course. We all circle back to our teenage writings, don't we? Yet I scarcely recognised the writer. He was a bit loose, a bit wild, no more than conventionally dedicated, no more than averagely gloomy about the human condition and had no idea what was coming his way. He was so *innocent*.

Now only one part of that prior innocence survived. I channelled such energies as remained into becoming Jaz's defender. I committed to honouring his memory. I idealised him. I imbued him with qualities far nobler than mine. I fastened on the idea of his death as an accident. When people asked, I insisted on the misfortune of, in what we used to call 'the country town with traffic lights', being killed running them. I became, in fact, something of a devotee of randomness. Chance ruled. Luck determined. Cock-up owned conspiracy every time. Could we not see that everything was a fluke, that we were all helplessly at the mercy of the fates?

Now I have read 'Jasper Haigh Reports', with its veiled speculations that my brother accelerated into an intersection about to be crossed by an oncoming car, I recognise I may have leaned too far and perhaps knew all along. After all, what I chose in my campaign of renunciation was itself a kind of slow suicide: I took my brother's eating disorder and cubed it. By 1989, when I moved to the UK, essentially to get out from people's scrutiny in order to suffer in exile, my weight plunged to 42 kilos. On reflection, perhaps I did suspect that there

had been a degree of volition in my brother's death, and perhaps I did fear the tendency was in me also. Suicide lurks in my work too: my first biography was of a gifted sportsman who took his own life; I can think of another dozen of my books in which suicide features.

You need not set out to kill yourself to do yourself in. You can run risks. You can abandon cares. Perhaps if your senses are dulled by apathy, you crave a jolt to live. Perhaps if your connectedness to others is attenuating, death offers a dark communion. I almost got there myself, in a sequela to Jaz's death. I returned to my tiny, filthy studio flat in Balham and found that I had lost those photobooth images I had taken on the morning of his death. I was inconsolable. My litany of failures was now just too long to be redeemed. I stood in a high window, five storeys up. I couldn't bear to live any longer, but I couldn't, to a slightly greater degree, bear to leave my mother with another corpse of another son. I stopped my ears to the siren song of self-annihilation. At length I stepped down and settled for years more suffering. Sometimes the question arises: is there anything you've lost in your life that you would dearly love back? I lie and say no because it is too hard to explain what I feel for this strange photographic memento of my pain on 13 August 1987, this vanished *vade mecum*.

Though I struggle to articulate it, I wanted in these years nothing more nor less than to disappear. If everything was perishable, if nothing was secure, then why not dwindle away? I deserved no better; I would scarcely be missed. I would leave behind my work as a grudging concession. My work I could stand by; my work I could defend. It was the part of me that was good; it was the only part of me I could live with, and that sense has quietly, naggingly persisted. Go on, read me: it's all I have to offer. The rest you wouldn't like. Trust me. You don't want to find out.

5

I have picked this up again after putting it aside to draw breath, to consider what next. I can see that the theme, such as it was, is expended, like a rocket's first stage, having served the purpose of getting me started; yet the need cloys and claws. Some years ago, I read about Wilfred Bion, who pursued psychoanalysis after watching fellow soldiers grapple with the traumas of the Western Front. Bion noted how deliberately some of them avoided understanding their experiences and emotions: he dubbed this state 'minus K'. I wondered at the time whether I had arrived at a similar mentality—and, of course, immediately put the thought to flight. But the trouble with a retentive memory, for I'm lumbered with one, is an inability to do this entirely, and something in me now seems to have shifted that chronic resistance to self-inquiry. So I'm going to stagger on, with the excuse that this is no memoir: this is less a geology of my life than a core sample. There are no famous people; there are no funny stories; there are, above all, no PBMs. But there will be no avoiding and excusing either. There has been enough.

The first five years after my brother's death were the worst. I gradually, determinedly, reduced my life to a state as near death as possible. The few family photographs—they are painful to look at—show me emaciated, etiolated, almost zombified. Still, I worked. How I worked, in a state of near catatonia that was strangely disinhibiting. If everything is equally fearful, then nothing is overwhelmingly fearful. If everything is hopeless, then the completion of your task can make things no worse. I took a new job, which I did well. If it was not much, it was at least something.

I did, then, get better, or at least got older. Marcus prescribed the newly available Prozac, and the icy grip of trauma gradually relented, replaced by the grind of long-term, low-level endogenous depression. I remain ambivalent about the efficacy of medication. In the immediate aftermath of Jaz's death, I could feel myself buckling beneath my burdens, desperate to set them aside. In some ways, medication nourished the belief I could endure them, to the extent they became part of me, like a hunch or a limp, recalling William Styron's memorable phrase that the depressed are society's 'walking wounded'.

Still, medication helped break my cycle of anxiety and anhedonia. I remade friends. I relearned partaking in pleasures, even if the wondering whether I deserved them never vanished altogether, and the calculus of permission was invariably tortuous. Permission never, for instance, extended as far as holidays. Everywhere I travelled there had to be a work component. And that work had to be performed as ascetically and austerely as possible. I hid so successfully behind my work it hardly felt like hiding at all. My first book, published in 1987, had contained an author's photograph and a lengthy, jokey bio; my second, published in 1993, offered no more than the brusque 'Gideon Haigh is a Melbourne journalist'. Leave me alone, I'm busy.

I saw benefit in my professional independence and freedom, but they were hardly the only reason I became a freelance journalist in 1995. It left me dependent on nobody. The best way to avoid being let down was to resist being picked up. It left me to regulate my schedule—the necessitous life of the freelance justified a regime without relief. I often felt tired. I was occasionally exhausted. But I had a purpose, however grim. I was making something of my chances, the chances denied others, the chances *denied Jaz*. Because there *did* lurk a yearning to make my life doubly meaningful in order to redeem his forgone opportunities. Because he couldn't,

I would. If there was a responsibility lying round, I would pick it up. If there was a stand to take, I would take it. I again started considering myself strong, fortunate and, at any rate, alive.

The objective was neither success nor wealth. Nor did I anticipate that what I did would change much about my life. A friend, a seriously fine novelist, gave up writing a decade ago, probably at the top of her form. She could, she explained, no longer handle the disappointments of publication—the false excitement, the hope that this would be the book that changed things, the repeated discovery that it wasn't. I totally understood this because I had taken the precaution of building in and allowing for failure. I never expected the act of publication to be personally transformative; I was merely trying to keep things going that little longer. If that put a cap on the satisfaction I derived from my work, it at least caused me minimal pain, while the combination of genuinely following my interests and not caring what followed had the tendency to concentrate my energies in the creative phase. By the time one book came out, I was usually well down the track of the next.

It is surprisingly easy, after a while, to go on working, when nobody is saying not to, when there is always something to do. The nature of my career made summer a period of peak demand, and I simply never made provision to catch up. But I grew a bit angry too—a frequent companion to and displacement of depression. I was seen as uncompromising. I became known for not suffering fools. I seethed when I encountered what I saw as the slipshod, the sentimental, the meretricious, the self-congratulatory—a handicap in a trade that is full of these things. I developed a strong sense that this was a world in which the wrong people prospered and the wrong people suffered—not actually a bad attribute for a journalist, if sharpened in my sense to an almost unreasonable degree. But I delivered and delivered and delivered. Fifty-one books! I never missed a deadline. I presented most manuscripts early. I left publishers and editors with nothing to do. But if, as I perceived it, they let me down, I never forgave them. I talked back, I dug in, I fought my corner as though my life depended on it—and maybe, in a way, it did, because work loomed so large in my thinking.

There is a passage towards the end of Narayan's *English Teacher* where the eponymous character, still grappling with the loss of his wife, sits down to write a resignation letter—and writes and writes, pouring out page after page of frustration at his general embattlement. 'I am up against the system,' he rails, 'the whole method and apparatus of a system of education which makes us morons, but efficient clerks for all your business and administrative offices.' At length he pulls himself up and settles for 'Dear Sir, I beg to tender my resignation for personal reasons'. I struggled to pull myself up. Just as the professional was personal, the personal grew professional. I sometimes earned respect for the 'courage' of my stances. But courage is when you feel you have something to lose and risk it. I never felt I had anything because I *was* alone—split off, unmoored, unresolved. Even when my life stabilised sufficiently for adult relationships, I subtly resisted, if not resented, anything restful, anything domestic. And to a high-functioning depressive personality, giving and receiving love comes hardest. Me? You love *me*? Oh, you don't want to do that. I'll always find a fault, push you back, let you down, depending on how my fear of intimacy flexes with my horror of loneliness. I wasn't an inconsiderate boyfriend; I wasn't a terrible husband; I have tried hard, very hard, as a father. But this has always been accompanied by a nagging dread that these are not things I am good at and that sooner or later this will emerge. I was present,

I was reliable and I was loyal, but I was never, I think, entirely *available.*

I tried therapy, of course. That perennial admonition: 'You should see someone'. But they were only ever someones, never anyone in particular. I was also held back by finding neither myself nor my problems all that interesting. I mean, they were hardly beyond my rational comprehension, and most people, it seemed, had far more to complain of than me. Comparatively I thought myself lucky, maybe even undeservingly so. I knew by rote what to say about my father, my brother, others who had come and gone. So I would grow bored. I would look down on myself and think: who is this guy and why doesn't he shut up? There was nothing to be learned from these sterilised encounters, these mimes of candour. I thought of David Foster Wallace's 'Depressed Person'—not only in 'terrible and unceasing emotional pain' but also stricken with 'the impossibility of sharing or articulating this pain', which became 'a contributing factor in its essential horror', and which sounded about right.

Time passed. The ranks of 1987 thinned. My grandmother, aunt and uncle died; likewise Julie and Ann. Essentially only my mother and I remained of the circle of that morning, and we had an unspoken understanding about those things at which we were to be getting on. Now retired, my mother had a full diary of voluntary work; now freelance, I blocked out every unallocated hour. Only now and again would it get too real. My father's and brother's birthdays, for example, fall on consecutive days, always in Melbourne Cup week. Not a sociable person anyway, I have always tended to go to ground around this time. I recall in 2004 realising that Jaz had been dead as long as he had been alive. I was

enjoying a movie called *Jesus of Montreal*. At the climax, the main character dies and his organs are harvested; there is a scene in which a patient awakes, gasping, with the benefit of his corneas. I burst into tears and fled the cinema. Fortunately I was alone; and being alone, as always, was a state of comparative safety.

The world of the bereaved is not merely sad but dangerous. It is full of cues, of snares, of jagged edges. My mother told me recently, for example, that she never fails to note on television the appearances of the sports journalist Rebecca Maddern—daughter of Wendy, the unlucky other driver in the collision, blessedly unharmed. 'I didn't know you knew the driver's name,' I said. 'I have always known the driver's name,' she replied evenly.

~

'You should see a grief counsellor,' urged a well-meaning friend recently. But this confuses grief and loss. Grief is crushing and bitter, but ultimately perishable. Loss abides. Loss is experienced in that moment when your direct involvement in what you are doing breaks for whatever reason, when you look around for that significant person you knew and realise all over again they're gone, when you reproach yourself for forgetting even as you shrink from remembering. I have worked hard at honing that capacity for direct involvement so as to avoid those moments. But, as Lewis said, loss spreads 'a vague sense of wrongness, of something amiss' over everything in your life. Even in those phases where you feel content, it is always out there lurking, poised to compound life's other inevitable losses.

D and I had been friends for fifteen years when we became a couple, very much at her initiative, as I could hardly compute that such a magnetic, talented and beautiful woman could be attracted to me. I was entirely captivated by her and although she lived in Sydney, it came as a revelation. D knew my history. D knew of loss. She was nonetheless an optimist, a celebrator of life, who poked loving fun at my occasionally acrid reflections on the culture and the mores. 'Ornery', she called me; I liked that. We did many great things together, including overseas travel: her love of comfort modified my limits of personal austerity; her flair for care squeezed my heart. One day when I was staying with her, I awoke with a blocked ear; in fact, the ear had been blocking regularly for months. My attitude was that under such circumstances you soldiered on; such was my incapability of doing anything for myself. Unbidden, D booked a doctor's appointment, sat in on the treatment, helped with the medication. I simply had no idea such kindness was possible; even now I feel tearful thinking of it.

So D was good for me, if also, at times, terrible, because she was volatile, possessive and controlling. She cared a great deal about what 'people' thought; I, sometimes self-defeatingly, did not. She wore her emotions on the outside, a coat of many colours; mine hung mainly inside, an all-black wardrobe. She never lost the conviction that our attachment was asymmetrical, that she loved me more than I her, which she expressed through cyclonic rages in response to innocent gestures and happenings: my wording of an acknowledgement to her, my taking a train to her place rather than a taxi, my mention of an ex's name, my walking with my daughter rather than her, my wearing something my mother had given me. These confrontations were never resolved or regretted; merely outlasted. Few have treated me more kindly, or, at times, more cruelly.

Yet being in the vicinity of someone almost obsessively in touch with their feelings is an injunction to consider one's own. It was only thanks to D that I was able to read Richard Beard's book and to revisit Canning Street, experiences from which I benefited even if I couldn't share them yet. D's confidence enabled me to write a book about N, a survivor of incestuous abuse: me and trauma again, part the millionth, but empowering too. N was an immensely damaged woman whose life had been destroyed by her father's unspeakable sexual tyranny, and who had been utterly failed by the welfare apparatus. It was good public service journalism; it also tapped my bottled-up resentment of those who had let Jaz down. *Go home, Mr Haigh. It doesn't get any better.*

Then came COVID, qualitatively different for me in Melbourne to D in Sydney, but difficult for everyone. Penned up in my 5-kilometre radius, dinned by the Daily Dan, watching my daughter C's education unravel, hearing my mother endure isolation from both of us, not to mention trying to eke out a freelance journalist's living—what else could possibly go wrong? My relationship. I was not where I should have been, with D. Talleyrand was right to observe that 'he who is absent is wrong'. Alone in my head, I stewed over D's complaints about my insufficiency of devotion and my gouts of negativity. I started doubting myself. For even when we were together, there would emerge little tensions, dissonances.

D, for example, wanted to teach me to ride a bike. I had never tried, pleading always that I was clumsy, had poor balance, liked walking. I knew in my heart that the inability was an echo of childhood. I was the boy who never wanted anything who became the 'husband' that did without. I never asked for a bike, unsure we could afford it; my brother, more healthily, asked, confident we could. I didn't experience any dissatisfaction about this at the time or even afterwards. But it had turned into an artefact of life with Jaz. In a favourite photo of us, I am standing while he sits on his bike. It was how I saw us, a natural juxtaposition and contrast, except I

knew it had become nothing of the sort—it was the aimless continuation of a learned helplessness. So I did, with D's encouragement, learn, while never quite feeling comfortable, and never quite losing the sensation it was not quite for me. I almost cannot get over how ridiculous this makes me sound.

D next wanted me to try driving, which I had also always deprecated. I was a good passenger, I would say airily; I was skilled at cadging lifts; I was an advocate of public transport. But men drive, don't they? It is a standard masculine capability. Not doing so is a kind of self-emasculation. So, for D, I fell in with the idea. Maybe I needed to conquer my aversion; maybe I should equip myself in order one day to teach my daughter. Except as I progressed through the theory, I sensed myself slow walking. I found excuses. I sought distractions. I finally gained my L-plates, posed with them, tried to look triumphant. And then, after a lifetime in the passenger seat, I got behind the wheel of D's car. It was far, far harder than the bike. In the driver's seat, it seemed as if the roads had narrowed by half, my clothes were on back to front and my shoes on the wrong feet. I felt trapped. The steering wheel felt inches from my chest. I was crowded by instrumentation, plagued by pedals. I was genuinely transported back to that police lot: the crushed driver's side of that Telstar across which I had leaned, reaching for the glove box. I had never understood until that day in 1987 how cars collapse on impact, never grasped how they could contract to spaces in which survival was impossible. Now, even in D's supersafe BMW, I felt claustrophobic. My back prickled with sweat against the seat. I flinched from the accelerator under my foot. I was frightened and, frankly, ashamed, at having turned another kindness into a self-torture.

Such ingrained superstitions were hardly the only reasons the relationship fluctuated. There remained that emotional mismatch between my autonomy and D's insecurity, my asperity about things and hers about … well, me. We had phases of great contentment, of seemingly deep connection. I relaxed with her probably as much as I had with anyone, while always knowing that the mood could turn in an instant. Which is how it ended. Five years into our relationship, a week after she addressed me in a birthday card as 'the love of my life' and 'the handsomest man in the world', and a day before I was to join her on holiday, D severed all contact.

Well, of course it made sense. It figured. And I was the perfectly resigned cuckold. D, I could see, was in a hurry to be happy. I had failed to keep pace and fallen away. I wasn't bitter. I didn't complain. I just quietly despaired—that old habit of underreaction to emotional upheaval, offset by those overreactions to transitory annoyances. And I worked. I buried myself in it. I wrote a book in three weeks and it was … good. I spent thirteen weeks working overseas, and it was … bad. So I quit my job. I could be one thing or another, unhappy in life or unhappy in work, and the latter was easier to change. I threw myself into a new book, with a second book to run alongside it.

The sorrow would not be effaced. A lover, a friend, a future gone so suddenly without farewell or explanation. I could not escape the likeness: this felt less a break-up than a widowhood. It wasn't as though D had left me; it was as though she had died. It was another *total loss.* So I simultaneously mourned everything in my life and could not stop. The irony is that my love, presumed so dour and conditional, long outlasted hers, so passionate and incandescent. It needed mercy killing, the excruciating slow poison of what had felt like the best part of me. And when, at last, I was finally truly bereft, when everything was somehow horrifying, and in the knowledge I could sink no lower, I commenced this reckoning. So here we are.

6

Domain

And there we conclude. Lewis finished *A Grief Observed* because he ran out of manuscript books: 'I resolve thus to let this limit my jotting. I will not start buying books for the purpose'. Sorrow, he decided, is a history, and 'if I don't stop writing that history at some arbitrary point, there's no reason I should ever stop'. My restriction is the patience with myself. Having come so belatedly to this exercise, I am additionally unwilling to let it go on forever. That was the point—not so much the writing, which has been raw, as the finishing, which must be rapid, pruned of memoir's usual self-pardonings and self-protections.

I'm honestly not sure what I have achieved—it is too early to tell. Having again lost my emotional bearings I have at least gone looking for them. Having at last official records to guide me has helped render more coherent the chaos of vivid impressions in my mind. And having failed to equip myself to teach C to drive I can, perhaps, teach her something else. Her latest obsession is genealogy. We subscribe to all the major sites; we will spend hours rummaging in digital catalogues and archives, finding clues, unravelling mysteries. No father has ever been prouder than when C, having watched me do it, ordered her first death certificate—it was a true 'she's leaving home' moment. C is doing family trees for her friends, my friends, my mother's friends. She's done ours, and will at intervals return to add here, prune there. As I look indulgently over her shoulder at the screen, I occasionally see a virtual tile slide past: *Jasper Haigh 1969–1987.* She never knew my brother, but he is part of her story. If she ever reads this, she may understand something of the uncle she never knew.

Does my life since Jaz's death make sense? Maybe a little more on the page than in my head. Nor am I afraid of holding this to the light. I've resumed, in a way, what I committed to in 1987—not looking away, not letting myself off. The only difference is I've dropped the façade of being fine. I'm not fine; I've never really been fine. And there is a solace in abandoning that pretence, in confronting and owning my accumulated failures, vulnerabilities and even motivations. Because it occurs to me that had Jaz lived, I might not still be doing what I have now done for forty years. His loss has gone on providing a powerful impetus, emotional as well as intellectual succour. I feel more strongly about it than ever. As for the rest of my life, I don't know. And I have no idea what happens next.

Afterword

The bulk of *My Brother Jaz* was written in a 72-hour stretch during 2024's Sydney Test match. I sent it to my mother, asking if she was comfortable with my publishing it; typically, she said that they were my words and that she had no wish to interfere with what I had to say. I posted it on my Substack, *Cricket Et Al*, on 10 January. To something I had always wanted to write, but had suspected I never would, there was an instant and a very warm response. I had always known it, but many people bear pasts that are, for whatever reason, difficult to share. I was honoured that, privately, they shared them with me.

So intense was my sense of urgency about *My Brother Jaz*, I had not at that stage even read through what I'd written, and I worried it was a bit of a mess. On a Saturday morning some weeks later I appended a slightly tidier conclusion—first time round, I'd simply been too exhausted from lack of sleep. By then I had been contacted by some publishers with a view to this book. For the support of my friend Foong Ling Kong of Melbourne University Publishing, I am enormously grateful. I thank others for their interest too.

The quote from Amis is on page 27 of *Experience* (Jonathan Cape, London, 2000); the quote from Narayan is on page 179 of *The English Teacher* (Mandarin, London, 1990); David Foster Wallace's 'The Depressed Person' is quoted from *Harper's*, January 1998, pp. 57–64; the quotes from CS Lewis's *A Grief Observed* (Harper, San Francisco, 1996) are from pages 5, 35 and 59–60; the epigraph is from page 28. I warmly commend you to Richard Beard's *The Day That Went Missing* (Vintage, London, 2017), which I also cite. Richard was kind enough to message me after 'My Brother Jaz' appeared on Substack, and I look forward to us playing cricket together one day.

Naturally, people have asked since whether writing *My Brother Jaz* has 'helped'. All I can say is that not writing it had not rendered life any more liveable. Something else: I was not to know at the time, but forthcoming events would also prove challenging, so it was useful, perhaps, to have set to one side what I was already carrying—the opportunity denied my brother.